AWESOME!

An Inside Guide To
WRESTLING SUPERSTARS

AWESOME!

An Inside Guide To
WRESTLING SUPERSTARS

by Joe Bosko

Parachute Press, Inc.

TABLE OF CONTENTS

THE HISTORY OF WRESTLING

Wrestling is a basic animal instinct. Kittens, dogs, monkeys, and children all enjoy fighting freestyle. And that's the basic motive behind wrestling's eternal popularity. It's the world's oldest spectator sport. Early artifacts from ancient civilizations, such as Mesopotamia, ancient Egypt, China, Japan, and India, prove that wrestling has been around as long as any other part of life.

For over five thousand years, Sumo wrestling has been fantastically popular in Japan. Sumo is a bigger deal in Japan than the Super Bowl is here! Sumo festivals are held four times a year for fifteen days, and the matches last from nine in the morning to six at night.

Sumo is more like football blocking than professional wrestling, though. Wrestlers usually weigh between 300 and 400 pounds and start training at five in the morning every day, which means slamming into tree trunks! Wrestlers try to shove their opponents outside a ring, and resort to anything they can to win. They'll lift, slap, trip, or throw their opponents.

Unlike pro wresting, though, dirty tricks like punching or deliberately trying to injure an opponent aren't allowed. The honor and tradition of Sumo are so important that no Sumo wrestler would ever think of breaking the rules. In some ways, it's too bad modern professional wrestling isn't more like Sumo!

The ancient Greeks were the first to fight in a style close to what we now call pro wrestling. At first the Greeks wrestled freestyle and did whatever it took to win. In 900 B.C., the legendary King Theseus set down rules to keep the fights fair.

The ancient Romans probably had an even bigger influence on today's pro wrestling. Thousands of people attended gladiator matches, during which the crowd would go bananas as one fighter went up against another. The Romans refined the Greek style of wrestling and created the Greco-Roman style of wrestling, which is still practiced today in Olympic competition.

After the fall of the Roman empire, in the fifth century, wrestling festivals declined. But wrestling refused to die. Small-time countryside bouts became very popular, even though the huge arenas of the Empire were forever silent.

When Europe emerged from the Dark Ages, and civilization began to reappear in Europe, wresting reappeared in a big way. Competitions between wrestlers were like wars! Royal titles, large estates, and even entire armies were bet on the outcome of wrestling bouts. Once, in the early sixteenth century, King Francis the First of France and King Henry the Eighth of England got so worked up over a match that was taking place, they began to wrestle with each other! (The match ended before a winner was declared.)

When the New World, America, was discovered by Europeans,

wrestling crossed the ocean. But early settlers learned that American Indians also liked to wrestle! European wrestlers learned new techniques from their Indian counterparts. A new, American style of wrestling, called freestyle, was born.

By the nineteenth century, traveling circuses and carnivals featured wrestling as part of their entertainment. A cash prize would be offered to anyone who could beat their champion. This was the origin of America's pro wrestling mania. Men of all sizes and descriptions would go after the prize of "The Toughest Man in Town." Money wasn't the only consideration; the men who took up the challenge, like today's pro wrestlers, were after fame—not just the bucks. And if you were man enough to beat the traveling champion, who knows? Maybe you would get an offer to become the new wrestling champion!

After the Civil War, national wrestling championships, along with national boxing championships, were held around the country. One of the first champions of the 1800s was Tom Jenkins, a giant man with only one eye. He used a style close to what we now call professional wrestling. One of his toughest opponents was Frank Gotch. The first official pro wrestling rivalry was born as they fought for the official title of World Champ.

Baseball, movies, and newspapers became popular in the early part of the twentieth century, but nothing got in the way of wrestling's popularity. One of the biggest stars at that time was Ed "Strangler" Lewis. He was a huge man, with massive hands, who warmed up for bouts by popping basketballs and footballs in his hands. The Strangler was so popular that it was many years before he was forgotten. One of pro wrestling's few drawbacks is that its past heroes aren't as famous as in other sports. After all, Ed Lewis was as important to wrestling as Babe Ruth was to baseball. But how often do you hear about this great champion today?

After the Strangler's retirement, wrestling went through a dull period. But then television came along, and wrestling, like the rest of the world, was never the same again.

The star who made TV wrestling so popular was Gorgeous George. If not for Gorgeous George, pro wrestling might have disappeared from the American scene. No one had ever seen anything like him before. He would strut into the ring as his theme song, "Pomp and Circumstance," played in the background. Before he entered the ring, his personal valet, Jeffry, dressed in a dinner robe, would spray the ring, referee, and opponent with perfume, so everything smelled right for Gorgeous George. Jeffry would then remove George's robe, a flashy, flowing velvet black robe with gold sequins. George's hair was dyed—sometimes blond, sometimes blue—but always something different, and wrapped in a net. He would remove the net, take bobby pins out of his hair, and throw them to the crowd. He was wrestling's first true villain, the man everyone loved to hate. Before anyone knew what was happening, millions of people around the country bought TV sets so they could tune in to Gorgeous George's outrageous act.

Gorgeous George was TV's first superstar. He wasn't the greatest wrestler of all time; in fact, he wasn't even a good wrestler. But by bringing showmanship into the game, he influenced every single wrestler who came afterward.

After Gorgeous George, many champions have come and gone. Some of them have been forgettable, while others remain in our consciousness, like all great TV stars. Bruno Sammartino, "The Living Legend," instantly comes to mind as the greatest champion in pro wrestling history. Bruno held on to his title for over ten years. From May 17, 1963, when he whipped "Nature Boy" Buddy Rogers for the championship, to December 10, 1973, when Stan Stasiak beat him, Bruno held the heavyweight championship. He was wrestling's ambassador, a man so popular that many fans felt the sport lost everything when he retired. Luckily, "The Living Legend" can be heard as a commentator on WWF telecasts.

Cable television provided the next big boost to wrestling's incredible popularity. That, and Vince McMahon's brilliant move in the late 1970s. McMahon moved wrestling into the time slot opposite *NBC's Saturday Night Live*. At that time, *Saturday Night Live* wasn't as popular as it had once been. Before long, wrestling took over Saturday night entertainment. And when pro wrestling provided cable TV stations with cheap, fun entertainment, with incredible ratings to boot, it became a media phenomenon. Before you could say "Hulk Hogan," wrestlers were bigger TV stars than soap opera stars, stand-up comedians, or talk show hosts.

Although some wrestling fans are turned off by the over-commercialization of their favorite sport, it has remained popular to this day. No matter how glitzy, respectable, or ridiculous the sport of wrestling becomes, there's always been a strange fascination with it. It goes back to the animal instinct. Kittens, dogs, monkeys, and children all fighting freestyle. The anarchy. The disorder. The triumph of good over evil. Wrestling is as basic as a ham sandwich.

And twice as much fun!

HULK HOGAN

"I'm run ragged. I wish they could clone me, so I could be in all the places I have to be."

—Hulk Hogan

There aren't many sports heroes who achieve the title of "legend" while they're still in their prime. In baseball, Don Mattingly has become a legend. In football, there's Walter Payton. And in basketball, Larry Bird and Kareem Abdul-Jabbar can be considered legends in their own time.

But when it comes to wrestling, there's only one legend in the sport today—Hulk Hogan. Hulk Hogan IS pro wrestling right now. He dominates mat wars the way the Beatles took over the pop charts in the sixties.

Hulk Hogan's popularity is legendary. Unbelievable. AWE-

SOME! When the Hulk took a vacation from wrestling from the "Mecca of Maul," New York's Madison Square Garden, for five months in1985, they had their biggest drop in attendance in over twenty years. If not for Hulk Hogan, wrestling could fade away the way pro soccer did in America when the legendary Pele left the sport.

Lots of wrestling experts and ring professionals have studied the Hulk Hogan myth to find out why he's one of the most popular people in the world today. Some experts point to his rugged good looks as the focal point of Hulkamania. Wrestling critics say it's his massive six-foot-three-inch, 307-pound body that attracts the crowds. Still others in the field say it's all a big hype, and that Hogan is popular just because he's the champ, and that as soon as he loses, the fans will cheer the next titleholder as wildly as they applaud Hulk Hogan today.

But the fans know the real reason for the Hulkster's fanatical following. It's his courage, heart, and pure wrestling ability. The fans have seen Hulk come back from impossible odds, time after time, to snatch victory from the jaws of defeat.

Certainly, no wrestler has ever come from a background like Hulk's. He was born on August 11, 1953, in Augusta, Georgia. His real name was Terry Gene Bollea. Even then, he was something special—he weighed ten pounds and ten ounces at birth! His parents knew they had a future athlete in the family.

When the Hulkster was just a little tot of three years old, his family moved to Tampa Bay, Florida. He was no different from any other kid who grew up in the sixties—he was interested in baseball, comic books, and rock'n'roll. At age 12, he was a star pitcher on the Tampa Bay Little League Championship team. A pro baseball career just wasn't in the cards for him, though—two years after his team won the state championship, he suffered torn ligaments in his right arm. His future as a baseball pitcher was over.

But, even then, the Hulkster was not the type to sit around feeling sorry for himself. He just picked up his guitar and decided to become a famous rock star. By the time he was in high school, he was playing bass guitar for local Tampa Bay groups.

But Hulk knew that a career as a successful rock'n'roller was as likely as winning the lottery. So in addition to playing with a slew of rock'n'roll groups while he attended the University of South Florida, he studied music and business administration, just in case he didn't make it big as a rock star.

The Hulkster, still known as Terry, was playing bass in a Tampa nightclub in 1973 when he was discovered by two wrestling promoters, former NWA champ Jack Brisco and his brother, Jerry. They saw some raw material in the giant rock'n'roller, and asked him if he had ever considered going into pro wrestling. Although he said "No way, dude!" at the time, he thought about it later. After all, being a wrestling star is sort of like being a rock star, right?

Several weeks later, he ran into the Briscos again. He decided to give pro wrestling a try. But wrestling is serious business! Before Hulk would go in the ring, he trained for six months with the great Japanese master, Hiro Matsuda.

His first professional match was in Tennessee, where he wrestled under the name of Terry Boulder. Early on, he even teamed with his brother Eddie (rumored to be none other than Brutus Beefcake). One big development in his life came when he moved to Venice Beach (better known as Muscle Beach), California, in the late 1970s. Although he spends all but two weeks a year on the road, he still calls Venice Beach his home. There, he was encouraged to build his body up to the super hulk-size it is today. Hulk also went through a name change. He became Sterling Golden, a villainous rule-breaker. It didn't help matters that his manager, "Classy" Freddie Blassie, encouraged him to pull any dirty trick to win. But Hulk was new to the profession. He didn't realize that you could obey the rules and win.

The Hulkster has admitted to his less-than-wonderful past, but he's not proud of it. "When I first started," he revealed, "I wasn't the greatest wrestler in the world, so I took a few shortcuts, took some cheap shots. But I found out that wasn't the way to get to the top. I don't think the bad guys could sell as many Hulk Hogan dolls as I have."

The biggest turnaround of Hulk's career came on September 17, 1981. He was wrestling in the AWA then, as Hulk Hogan, and was ranked third in their ratings. The popular Brad Rheingans, an ex-Olympic hopeful, was being attacked by the 400-pound Crusher Blackwell. Hulk saved Brad, and the fans realized that Hulk had given up his evil ways. For the first time in his career, Hulk Hogan received the cheers of the crowd.

But Hulk didn't help Brad so he could get a little cheap applause. "It made me sick to see an All-American kid, one who was supposed to go to the Olympics last year, get dumped by Blackwell for no reason at all," he said.

That was the end of his days as a rule-breaker and cheap-shot artist. From that point on, Hulk heard the cheers of the crowd wherever he went. And he responded. It was as if the cheers of the fans made him a new man.

Then came the biggest break in his career. He played Thunderlips in *Rocky III*, co-starring with Sylvester Stallone and Mr. T. At first, when the Hulkster learned that Stallone wanted him to star in a film, he thought it was a joke. But he soon took it seriously. And it paid off in a very big way!

After his role in his first feature film, Hulk continued to wrestle in the AWA, but failed to win a title belt. Although he was involved in several title matches, Hulk never managed to win the big one. Most savvy ring observers note that Nick Bockwinkel, the reigning AWA champ at the time, used a lot of trickery and deception to keep Hulk from winning the title. The fact that he couldn't get a fair shot at the title belt infuriated the Hulkster! So he moved to the WWF, where he became an instant sensation. Although some people say it was the inferior competition that got him his title belt, it was probably the politics of the situation that enabled Hulk to take over.

Then-champion Bob Backlund helped the Hulkster find his way through his first time around. That ironically led to a title bout for Hulk against the Iron Sheik, who had defeated Backlund.

When Hulk defeated the Iron Sheik on January 24, 1984, at Madison Square Garden, it was an event that went down in history. The Hulk was at his devastating best, wiping out The Iron Sheik in less than eight minutes. The most thrilling moment came when Hulk broke out of the Sheik's dreaded "Camel Clutch," a hold that no one had ever gotten out of before! The Hulkster not only broke the hold, but finished off the evil Sheik within seconds of breaking it. He became only the ninth champion in the long history of the World Wrestling Federation.

Since gaining the world championship, life has hardly been a bed of roses for Hulk. Greg "The Hammer" Valentine was the first "big name" bad guy that Hulk had to go against. Valentine threatened to break Hulk's legs, and many of his former opponents, fearful that "The Hammer" could back up his threats, tried to talk Hogan out of the match. It was then that it became apparent that Hulk Hogan was on a personal crusade to clean up wrestling. Perhaps because Hogan himself had once been a rule-breaker, he's taken it upon himself to police wrestling and keep the villains, cheap-shot artists, and bad guys from ruining the sport.

Shortly thereafter, Hogan faced one of the biggest opponents of his career—Big John Studd. Although he came close to losing the match, he not only won the match, but eventually body-slammed Studd, a feat that many thought impossible before Hogan proved otherwise.

For a short time, Hulk paired up with Andre the Giant, but their attempt at a partnership failed badly. Although the WWF tried to hush up the rumors, the Hulkster and Andre fought bitterly in their dressing room before many of their matches. It was a clash of the egos that could have ended in disaster. As one promoter said, "Even when they were supposedly friends, you could always feel the tension. They're an explosion waiting to happen."

The next notable opponent for the Hulk was The Magnificent Muraco. Hogan not only took care of Muraco, the "Beach Bum," but he also took the time to beat up Mr. Fuji, one of the nastiest managers in the game. Hulk was, once again, just cleaning up the sport. As Lou Albano, the now-retired manager, put it, "He's going to make a point. The point is you don't interfere when someone is wrestling. The minute you step over the line from adviser to participant, you had better be prepared to pay some heavy consequences."

Among the opponents Hogan faced in his first year of his title reign were David Schultz, Ken Patera, the Masked Superstar, and, in the closest decision perhaps of his career, Japanese hero Inoki. His first title defense in Madison Square Garden was against Paul "Mr. Wonderful" Orndorff.

Hulk Hogan helped put wrestling on the map with Wrestle-mania I. The Hulkster's tag team match with Mr. T, in which he defeated "Rowdy" Roddy Piper and Paul Orndorff, wasn't a classic match by any means, but it attracted celebrities from all over the world. Everyone from Billy Martin, Muhammed Ali,

Cyndi Lauper, and the late Liberace attended the festivities.

Hogan may be a great wrestler, good with the press, and even a good actor as well, but the one thing he hasn't done well throughout his career is pick tag team partners. His attempted partnership with Paul Orndorff was the biggest mistake he made in his career. But maybe that's one of the reasons Hulk is so well-loved—everyone can see that, as big and strong as he is, he's only human. But you can't blame Hulk. Although everyone can second-guess the Orndorff-Hogan tag team now, at the time, it was seen as possibly the most devastating ever. Orndorff may have ruined the team with his egomaniacal antics, but you can't blame Hogan for trusting his partner.

But let's forget his small, stupid mistakes. By Wrestlemania II, Hogan proved why he's been the world's champ for as long as most people can remember. Shortly before the event, Hogan went up against Randy Savage. At the time, his ribs were taped up, and he was fresh out of a hospital bed. Then the Hulkster had to face King Kong Bundy . . . in a steel cage match! As throughout Hogan's career, he performed the impossible. Bundy's avalanche move, in which all 446 pounds of his massive body slam into his opponent, didn't faze the Hulkster when he was driven into the ropes with it. It only made him MADDER! And before you knew it, he picked Bundy up and threw him into the mat with such force that every single fan in the arena jumped to his feet.

By now, Hulk Hogan was being recognized as the greatest wrestler of the decade, and perhaps of the century. And for good reason. His next "big name" opponent was none other than Andre the Giant. The same Andre the Giant who had never lost a match in his long, outstanding career. The same Andre the Giant whom Hulk had to meet in the epic "Clash of the Titans" match at the Pontiac Silverdome in Michigan, in front of millions.

18

It's a shame, really, that two great wrestlers like Hulk and Andre had to go against each other. The confrontation tore wrestling fans apart in a bitter argument over who would win. But the stage had been set. The feud was an old one. It wasn't as if Hulk and Andre were old friends. Their animosity toward each other was well-documented.

More than 93,000 fans packed the Silverdome to see the fight, and they weren't disappointed. Incredibly, Hogan was able to body-slam his seven-foot-five-inch, 520-pound opponent!

Sad to say, but there aren't a lot of mountains left for the incredible Hulk Hogan to climb. He's done about all there is to do. He's beaten every big-name opponent, every challenger, and anyone who might pose a threat to his reign as heavyweight champion of the world.

But that could be the true test for Hulk Hogan. The greatest heavyweight boxing champion of all time was Joe Louis, "The Brown Bomber," although his opponents were so awful that it became a bad joke every time he fought. He battled "The Bum of the Month Club." Any idiot foolish enough to risk life and limb against Joe Louis could do it.

But no one took anything away from Joe Louis. He fought everybody he had to fight. He beat anyone who would get in the ring and challenge his ability. And that is why Joe Louis is remembered as the greatest boxer of all time.

So it is with Hulk Hogan. He has not only beaten every challenger who's come his way, he's turned them into mincemeat. The bigger they are, the harder they fall. And now, the true test of his championship rule will come.

Can Hulk Hogan successfully defend what is probably the greatest career in wrestling history? I certainly wouldn't bet any money against it! After all, he's the hardest-working athlete in America today.

"It's like I've been telling kids: 'Train, say your prayers, eat your vitamins.' Since I've been livin' by that I've been doin' pretty good."

The biggest challenge for Hulk Hogan is Hulk Hogan. He has virtually no time to himself. He's working overtime on a movie about his life, while defending his championship, fulfilling endless press obligations, and doing volunteer work.

For instance, his mom and dad still live in Tampa, Florida, and although he finds the time to visit them, in spite of his busy schedule, it has to hurt the guy that he can't spend enough time with them. He'd like the time to visit more often.

And he hasn't found the time to settle down and get married. He's a clean liver and doesn't smoke or drink, or approve of people who do. His favorite drink is milk, "the breakfast of body slammers." He lives life as he does because, as he says, "It proves to all the little Hulksters out there that if you work hard and get to bed early, you can accomplish anything."

But at some time, Hulk has to slow down, find time for his own life, and settle down. No human being can be expected to maintain his crazy, hectic schedule. That's the hardest part to being a champion: not only do you have to beat your opponent in the ring, but you have to deal with everything outside of it— the endless interviews, public appearances, and autograph signings take their toll, even if you're Hulk Hogan. And don't forget, outside of that, Hulk has to find the time to train, and keep in top condition.

This is the toughest challenge for Hulk Hogan, which we will hear more and more about as the time comes near. Can he top Bruno Sammartino's incredible ten-year reign as heavyweight champ? Or is that ten-year title reign, like Joe DiMaggio's fifty-six-game hitting streak, an unbreakable record? Only time will tell.

ANDRE THE GIANT

"I'll be back!"

—Andre the Giant to Hulk Hogan

Wrestling, as everyone knows, has its share of BIG stars—but there's no question that Andre the Giant is the biggest. Just how big is he? Well, check out these stats:

Height—Seven feet five inches (Yes, we mean *seven*)

Weight—535 pounds

That makes him taller than the tallest centers in basketball— and twice as heavy as most heavyweight boxers. Andre really is a giant—that is a medical term for people whose growth is way beyond normal. True giants, like Andre, tend to be very tall and big even when they are babies. This condition often runs in families. It did in Andre's. His grandfather was a giant as well.

Being so big obviously has many advantages for a wrestler—but outside of the ring nearly everything is more difficult for Andre than it is for a normal-size person. Try to imagine having to sit on those tiny chairs you had in kindergarten, and you can picture what Andre goes through every time he tries to sit in a normal chair. Picture yourself trying to climb into a baby stroller, and you get some idea about how Andre feels about taxis. Or worst of all, just think how you would feel if every single person you met asked you the same question: "How does it feel to be so tall?"

It's a tough life, but Andre is used to it.

Andre's real name is Andre Rousimoff. He grew up in a small town in France, but he left home at a very early age to go his own way. When he was still a teenager, he met some wrestlers. They convinced him that his size would be a big plus in wrestling, and Andre decided to give it a try.

Andre took to the sport at once. With his enormous weight, Andre lacks quickness. (One writer said he moves with the speed of a glacier.) But he had strength and stamina and seemed to pick up a lot of wrestling smarts very fast. He traveled all over the world wrestling under the name Jean Ferre.

As you can imagine, wrestling fans were very eager to see him. A lot of people didn't believe he really could be *that* big. They came to see him the way people like to go to so-called freak shows. But they soon discovered that Andre had a lot to offer besides his size, and Andre became a crowd favorite.

It was Vince McMahon of the WWF who gave Jean Ferre his new name, Andre the Giant. He had recognized Andre had a certain kind of star quality that was as big as he is.

Andre's career has been a long and—up until very recently—a peaceful one. The only controversy around him was that there

22

were always people saying he should be disqualified because his size gave him an unfair advantage. Andre never took that talk seriously and always went out there and fought a fair fight. In his whole long career, he never lost a match—or won a title belt.

"I have had some championship bouts," he once explained, "but they either end at the time limit, or the champ gets himself disqualified, because they'd rather lose the match than the belt. I can't complain, though. This sport has given me everything I've ever wanted—friends around the world, contacts, everything."

Recent events changed all that, and cast a few shadows on Andre's once untarnished reputation. On the day he attacked Hulk Hogan on live television, shock waves spread throughout the world. Before you knew it, Bobby "The Brain" Heenan was managing Andre, and Andre faced Hogan in Wrestlemania III in a match for the championship.

Andre's legion of fans understood why Andre would do such a crazy thing—although Andre has always been extremely popular, and widely recognized as a great wrestler, he'd never won a title. And Andre's great career is winding to a close. He's wrestled for many, many years. Andre must realize that he has only a few years left to leave his mark on wrestling history.

The wrestling world watched in fascination when Andre lost to the Hulkster in Wrestlemania III. It was a shock to see him lose the first match of his long, wonderful career. But all good things come to an end—even Andre's long record of undefeated matches. But here's hoping that somehow, Andre will find a way to win that elusive Championship Belt before he decides to call it quits.

JESSE "THE BODY" VENTURA

"I'm the ONLY wrestler who has made a REAL rock 'n' roll record! And how many other wrestlers could get up on the stage in front of twenty thousand screaming maniacs and rock the place like it has never been rocked before?"

—Jesse "The Body" Ventura

"It's all a matter of class. Some people got it and some don't. Me, I've got an abundance of class."

—Jesse Ventura

A lot of wrestlers have appeared in movies. Primo Carnera, who wrestled in the forties and fifties, appeared in the giant ape movie *Mighty Joe Young*. Hulk Hogan appeared in *Rocky III*, but for the most part wrestlers haven't had starring roles. At least that's the way it was until Jesse "The Body" Ventura came on the scene.

24

His role in *The Predator*, starring Arnold Schwarzenegger, is dynamite! He literally steals the show. It's almost typecasting to have Jesse Ventura play the part of a big, tough guy who doesn't take garbage from anyone. As a wrestler, Ventura has always been a dangerous foe. He got his nickname, "The Body," from exactly where you might think—his body. Jesse is fanatical about his workouts, and pumps iron several times a week.

When you think about it, it makes sense that Jesse would make it big in the movies. His flamboyant style is right out of Hollywood. In fact, the 281-pound grappler has been called Mister Hollywood for his outrageous sense of style.

And he's considered by many to be the finest wrestling announcer in the business today. After his debut as an announcer in 1985, the raves poured in about his daring and aggressive style. Although not all of them came from Jesse, he probably is his own biggest fan. "The World Wrestling Federation knew the way to get ratings up was to get the greatest voice in the sport on the air," he said modestly. "I may not be the world champion—Hulk Hogan is, although that's only a matter of time—but there's no doubt I do the best commentary in wrestling."

If you don't mind Jesse's outspoken style, you'll find him quite interesting to listen to. He definitely presents a, to put it mildly, different point of view. For instance, he once said about the Junkyard Dog: "I think he's strong, tough, and real stupid. If brains were dynamite, The Junkyard Dog wouldn't be able to blow his nose." And that's one of the nicer things he said about him!

Jesse has been juggling several careers for quite some time. For instance, he took the rock world by storm when he released two records on the Twin-Tone Records label in Minneapolis. They became instant collector's items. His singing style has been described as "heavy metal rap," a nice way to say that what he has to say is more important that how he says it.

Jesse's rise in the world of rock music was nothing short of meteoric. When the rock group Mountain decided to re-form, they asked Jesse to perform in their video. And did he ever. Portraying a massive, medieval creature who battles to pull a guitar out of a rock, Jesse stole the show. The video crew couldn't believe their eyes when Jesse refused to wear any warm clothes in the frigid, eighteen-degree weather during the filming. "I had my body nicely oiled," he explained later. "I didn't want to mess it up."

Jesse's favorite moment in his rock career came when he met the legendary Ozzy Osbourne, and the two traded wrestling tips and musical advice for *Faces* magazine. "Meeting Ozzy Osbourne was a thrill," Jesse says. "I've been a fan of his since he was with Black Sabbath. His wild stunts have put a lot of madness into a lot of people—including some wrestlers, I'm sure."

Jesse may come off like a buffoon at times, but the fact is, he can back up most of what he says. Lord Alfred Hayes, who now works as a fellow ring announcer with Jesse, claims that he discovered Jesse in 1976. According to Hayes, Jesse once served in the navy's most elite fighting corps, the SEALS, in Vietnam. He proved his courage under heavy enemy fire many times. And, Hayes has revealed, Jesse once served as bodyguard for Mick Jagger of the Rolling Stones. Hayes was so impressed by Jesse's style and wrestling skill that he talked "The Body" into joining the ranks of pro wrestling.

The same guts and determination that got Jesse through the Vietnam War vaulted him to the top of the pro wrestling world. And now, those same qualities have helped him make a big splash in the movies. I'm not sure if Jesse will retire from wrestling to pursue a movie career, like Rowdy Roddy Piper, but if anyone can do it, Jesse "The Body" Ventura can.

LANNY POFFO

"Wresling-wise, Poffo is as good as I've seen. He has the moves, the smarts, and the desire to go on to great successes. With some solid management behind him, I see great things ahead for him.

—Bruno Sammartino

"There's a time and place for combat. The right way to let out aggression is through contact sports—in the ring, for example. The street is not the place."

—Lanny Poffo

One of the hottest souvenirs from the pro wrestling scene is a hand-signed Frisbee from Leaping Lanny Poffo. The Frisbees have one of Lanny's poems printed on them, and the autograph makes it a real collector's item. You see, Lanny's no ordinary wrestler—he's the "poet laureate" of the WWF! He usually recites some verse before one of his matches, and the WWF magazine has published many of his poems.

Lanny has prepared to be a wrestler his whole life. When he was only eight, he took gymnastics and dance classes. At Downers Grove North High School, near Chicago, Illinois, he was a catcher on the baseball team and also wrestled. Lanny became a pro wrestler as soon as he graduated in 1973. "I was not very good when I started," Lanny admits. "I often thought of quitting. I was getting beat pretty bad. I had my nose broken four times, my ankle broken twice."

Lanny's career had a rocky beginning, but he stuck with it for twelve and a half long years, and never gave up on the idea that he would make it big. "I never would have made it without my deep love for wrestling," he says.

It's easy to understand why he's been able to stick with it—wrestling is in his blood. His brother is Randy Savage, the Macho Man. And his father was very famous as the notorious ring villain, Angelo Poffo. Lanny gives his father a lot of credit for teaching him what it took to make it in the super-tough world of pro-wrestling. "My father is quite a guy," Lanny says. "In 1945, he set a world record by doing 6,033 consecutive situps. He still trains with an obsession. If I had half the heart he has, I'd be a superstar."

Although having a famous wrestler for a father helped Lanny get started, he never depended on his family name to make it easy. "My father's name opened some doors," Lanny says, "but once I got in the room I was on my own. I was still a high school punk, and it came slowly. My father took a lot of time with me. He taught me general lessons about wrestling and life."

Lanny's main loves in life are his wife and four-year-old daughter, wrestling, poetry, and medieval history. "Why did I become a fanatic?" says Lanny. "Because—courage, purity, honesty, humility, charity, fidelity, and diligence. These were the things that the knights sought for and fought for—and their unwerving loyalty to their king." Lanny's love for the age of King Arthur led him to buy a complete suit of armor, for an appearance on a television show, and he wore it on the air!

Lanny's complete dedication to his crafts, both poetry and wrestling, are amazing. Besides writing and reciting his own poetry, he can also recite thousands of poems by masters—Robert Frost, William Shakespeare, Edgar Allen Poe, and e. e. cummings—as well as Broadway musicals, the novel by F. Scott Fitzgerald *The Great Gatsby*, and John Kennedy's inaugural address.

He's as fanatical about his diet as he is about poetry. "Everything I've got is natural, he says. "I try to keep a natural diet—no drinking, no smoking, no drugs."

With the kind of dedication Lanny shows in everything he does, it's no wonder he's making it big in pro wrestling. In fact, it wouldn't be surprising if Lanny makes it all the way to the top and wins the WWF title belt. If perseverance and hard work could do it, he'd be the heavyweight champ already!

JAKE "THE SNAKE" ROBERTS

I'm called 'Snake' because I'll strike faster than a cobra and, yes, I'm just a little bit slimy!"
—Jake "The Snake" Roberts

There's a message that this man sends forth—even the meanest evildoer in the world can turn over a new leaf. Jake was once one of the most despised wrestlers in the game. He fought dirty, took the side of the villains, and tried to embarrass Hulk Hogan and other wrestlers on his World Wrestling Federation interview show, *The Snake Pit*. More than one wrestler was so scared of his snake, Damien, that they'd run right off the stage to get away from it.

But while Jake "The Snake," former bad guy, has reformed himself into a nice, respectable member of the wrestling community, he remains one of its most dangerous fighters as well. The master of the devastating wrestling move, the DDT, he shows absolutely no mercy to his adversaries.

Jake didn't begin his career as a bad guy by choice. His troubles began in 1982, when he crossed paths with Ken Sullivan, one of the most evil wrestlers in history. Kevin was a bad influence on Jake. He fed him a constant diet of steak and violent, bloody wrestling films!

There are even wilder stories about how Jake was brainwashed into being mean. Whatever the cause, it seemed to work. Jake won titles around the country and became a great wrestler. But his reputation was as bad as his behavior, which usually featured him dumping his snake on the face of a vanquished foe.

Eventually, Jake came to his senses. His basic good nature returned. Instead of wrestling heroes like Hulk Hogan or Junkyard Dog, he chose to fight villains like King Kong Bundy and Kamala. Instead of being hissed and booed he was cheered. Jake even cut a special segment against drug use for the World Wrestling Federation, where he tells everyone that "you don't need drugs to have fun." Even the rock star Alice Cooper hangs around with Jake nowadays. They have a lot in common—Alice also features a snake in his live performances!

Some people say that it really was Damien the snake that turned things around for Jake. The fact is that wrestling fans liked Damien. They thought he was—get this—cute. After all, snakes make good pets, and once you get used to them you find out that they're not good or evil creatures. Snakes, like most creatures, just do what they have to do to survive.

Just like Jake "The Snake."

Jake is a man who has often said that he'll "do what he has to do." With his invulnerable DDT maneuver, which he claims can "stun a man senseless," there seems to be no end in sight to his growing popularity. Standing at six-foot-five, and weighing 243 pounds, he has proved himself over and over again to be a winner.

Will success spoil Jake "The Snake"? As long as he concentrates on his success and not his popularity, he will continue to win, most experts agree. Many pick Jake "The Snake" to replace Hulk Hogan as WWF champion, once the aging Hogan retires, or loses his magic touch.

Jake calls himself "The Snake" because, as he puts it, "I strike faster than a cobra and I'm a bit slimy." Coming from a man who places a snake on the face of his fallen victims, it's hard to disagree with that point!

The Hulk is number one. The most famous and popular wrestler in the world holds high the championship belt after defeating Andre the Giant before a crowd of 92,000 in the Pontiac Silverdome.

U.P.I./Bettman Newsphotos

**Andre the Giant is a little choked up here at Wrestlemania II in a
20-man Battle Royal. No problem. He eventually won.**

**Hulk Hogan. His fans say he's a doll and
here he shows they are right. In his hands
is the popular Hulk Hogan action figure.
Isn't he cute?**

New York Post/Don Halasy

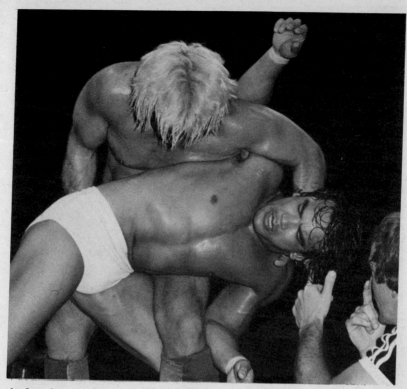

A classic match-up . . . Ric Flair against Ricky Steamboat. Guess you could call these shots the ups and down of wrestling.

The Road Warriors strut their stuff in a playground in New York's Central Park. I guess it's better than meeting them in a dark alley.

Whenever Flair and Steamboat meet, it's the fans who are the real winners.

California Doll is one of the most popular wrestlers in G.L.O.W. Don't let her delicate looks fool you, she's a tough competitor.

38

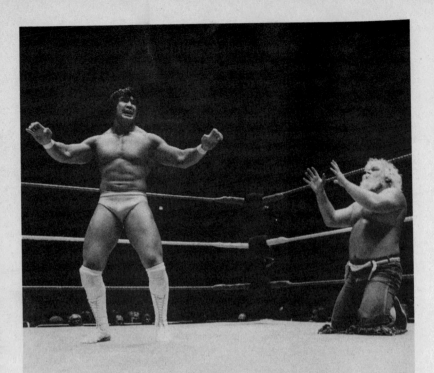

Ricky Steamboat celebrates after defeating Moondog Spot.

Is this a face to give you nightmares? King Kong Bundy intimidates his foe in the squared circle.

Sergeant Slaughter a little worse for the wear after a bout at the New Jersey Meadowlands.

Gorgeous Jimmy Garvin shows off his
 elegant form in the ring.

Kamala has been known as the kiss of death to many wrestlers, but this is ridiculous!

Is Hulk Hogan happy or sad? It looks like the agony of defeat—but it's really the thrill of victory!

New York Post/Michael Norcia

Hollywood and Vine look good and play hard!

**Hulk Hogan is one of the few people who
can look Andre the Giant in the eye.**

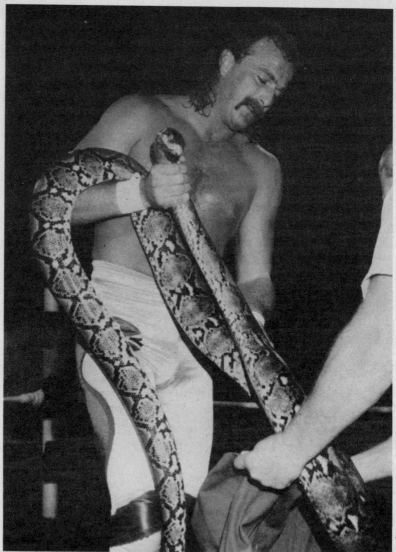

Jake the Snake shows Damien off to his admirers. Now that's a snake.

RIC FLAIR

"Many are called, but few are chosen."
—Ric Flair, describing himself

They call him Slic Ric—and the name certainly fits. In a world of brutes and animals, Ric Flair certainly looks like a class act. He's got the poise and the polish that a lot of wrestlers lack. And he's got the bank account to support his high-class tastes.

Ric Flair has recently been enjoying one of his most distinguished reigns as the NWA World Heavyweight Champion. Certainly not one to cover up his immense wealth, he not only owns a Rolls Royce, but he also has his own personal Lear Jet, complete with a full staff, to attend to his every need. Rick views his championship in a philosophical way. "Many are called," he says, "but few are chosen."

Over a long period of time, Ric has defended his title against every competitor who tried to take it away from him. In the first year of his third title reign, he has wrestled more men than Hulk Hogan would dream of.

Ric Flair is truly the real world's champ—the people's champion. Look at it this way. He pays five hundred bucks every time he gets his hair cut. He lives in the biggest house in town. And he does exactly what he wants to do for a living. In every sense of the word, he is a true hero!

Still, some people are turned off by the way he struts around the ring in feathers and furs. But no one ever suggests that he doesn't have the ability to back up his bragging. In fact, many of his fellow wrestlers have said that he is the hardest man to beat in the whole sport.

Ric's story is pretty amazing for one reason—he was nearly killed during a plane crash. His injuries were so severe that most people thought he'd never wrestle again. But within months, he was back in the ring. In fact, it was after the accident that his career really took off.

He teamed up with Greg "The Hammer" Valentine, and they won the NWA tag team belt. But then some of their unfair practices caught up with them, and they were stripped of the title.

So Ric went over to the WWF, where he teamed up with Ricky Steamboat. He was very popular in the WWF, but somehow he just couldn't resist taking some cheap shots and getting into trouble.

After a while, he went back to the NWA and became the heavyweight champion. Many ring experts believe that Ric Flair is the greatest wrestler in the world. They rank him above even Hulk Hogan!

Wrestling fans would love to see the two superstars face each other. But it probably won't happen. The rules don't allow the champion from one federation to challenge the champion of the other. But rules are made to be broken—or at least changed. Then the fans could see the ultimate match-up—Hulk Hogan against Ric Flair. Awesome!

MIDNIGHT EXPRESS

"I'm sick and tired of playing footsie with stupid wrestling promoters who will not see fit to grant a title shot to the Midnight Express."

—Jim Cornette

First, you have rude. Then comes very impolite, nuts, and finally, totally bananas. The Midnight Express are all of the above, and more. These guys would sell their grandmother for the price of a hamburger.

The Midnight Express are one angry tag team. Angry? You bet. If you were as ugly as they are, you would be too. Managed by the wild and crazy Jim Cornette, the team goes after one tag team belt after the other.

Just about every match with the Midnight Express is characterized by the Express creaming their opponents, followed by the cowardly Jim Cornette hitting the opposition over the head with his ever-present tennis racket. That infamous tennis racket comes in very handy to bait and distract other wrestlers. If that doesn't do the trick, Cornette has been known to throw a chair. Regardless, the Midnight Express, made up of "Loverboy" Dennis Condry and "Beautiful" Bobby Eaton, are clearly the best tag team in the NWA.

On the other hand, Cornette, whom the fans regularly call "wimp" or "weasel," usually can be found decked out in expensive, trendy clothing. If one didn't know better, they would swear he was a Wall Street banker, instead of a wrestler. At last look, if it wasn't for Cornette's tennis racket, the Midnight Express might not have won any wrestling matches. Cornette justifies the use of the racket by saying, "It's part of my image," or "Mother approves it."

Of course, with someone like Jim Cornette as manager, you'd figure the Midnight Express to be a pair of rulebreakers. And you wouldn't be disappointed. "Loverboy" Condrey has broken enough rules in his career to fill an encyclopedia. And "Beautiful" Bobby Eaton, once a scientific wrestler with a high regard for the sport of wrestling, picked up on his partner's method of operation as soon as they joined forces.

Although the Midnight Express's theme music is the theme from the movie of the same name, a sort of disco number, America's least-favorite tag team doesn't play up their rock 'n' roll connection. In fact, one of their arch-rivals is the Rock 'n' Roll Express, one of the most popular tag teams in the business today. But don't tell Cornette that. "I hate them," Jim Cornette said of the Rock 'n' Roll Express. "They are the lowest, silliest tag team I have ever seen!"

Whatever Cornette says, it doesn't matter once things get down to the mat wars. In fact, Cornette only gives ammunition to his foes with his inflammatory statements. And that only makes for a more hard-fought, exciting match.

But then, that's what wrestling is all about, isn't it?

ROAD WARRIORS

"My Warriors are machines."
—Precious Paul Ellering

"Somewhere deep down inside, there's a couple of human beings inside Animal and Hawk."
—Wahoo McDaniels

The Road Warriors may look weird, but don't tell them to their face—they think they look perfectly normal! Beyond their gimmicky makeup, though, the Road Warriors are great wrestlers. Managed by Precious Paul Ellering, Animal and Hawk are set to take over the world. Who can stop them?

Getting fame and recognition sure didn't come easy for this Terrible Twosome. The Road Warriors had to fight for every bit of their fame and recognition. It started on Chicago's South Side, where Animal and Hawk grew up. Faced with the everyday reality of the streets, they turned to weightlifting, determined to keep away from a life of crime and street gangs. As Animal put it, "You haven't many alternatives. Either be tough or be killed. Weightlifting turned me into a man. It gave me an identity."

Through strict, rigorous daily workouts, Animal and Hawk became bigger and stronger. Sure, no one kicked dirt in their faces, but they were tired of the city life and finally decided to move on. So they loaded up their car and began to drive. Although they had no destination in mind, they eventually stopped in Georgia. That's where their car broke down. As fate would have it, that's where Animal picked up a newspaper and came across an ad for pro wrestlers. He wasted no time at all in answering that ad right away—after all, what else could he do with no car?

Animal became obsessed with the idea of becoming a pro wrestler, and ranted and raved for weeks on end about how famous he would become, and about how much money he was going to rake in. "Imagine," he screamed, "getting paid to bang heads!" Unfortunately, in that first match, it was the Animal's head that got banged—OUCH!

Well, maybe getting his head banged did some good. For in that very audience was their future manager, Precious Paul Ellering. He was scouting talent. He saw a future star in Animal. And when he found out that there was a Hawk to go along with him, he knew he had hit the jackpot!

From that day on, the Road Warriors became the super-tough team they remain today—a single unit of utter destruction. Their matches are famous for harrowing elbow-smashes, killer forearm mashes, and their most lethal weapon, the power body slam. Their matches usually end in an uncontrollable eruption of general mayhem and senseless destruction. The main aim of the Road Warriors is to win, no matter how much pain they have to inflict on their opposition.

"Yeah, pain. Look up the word *pain* in the dictionary and you see a picture of us! Hahaha!" Hawk, of the Road Warriors has said.

Even though the Road Warriors have enjoyed phenomenal success, they cannot avoid controversy. Constantly, they are besieged by rumors of their breakup, or gossip that they'll soon be leaving their manager, Paul Ellering. The Warriors do little to end these rumors. If anything, they add to them.

Look at it this way, the Warriors have been together for a long time. They were bound to have some kind of internal trouble sooner or later.

The Legion of Doom may seem to be a unified group, but Paul Ellering seems to be more interested in his Wall Street business dealings, and Hawk and Animal can be found bickering and yelling at each other after matches. Whether they break up or not remains to be seen. Whatever the case, the world has not seen the last of Hawk and Animal, you can be sure of that!

THE GARVIN BROTHERS

"I'm the best wrestler in the AWA today."

—Jimmy Garvin

"What can I say? I'm on a roll. I'm ready for 'em. Bring 'em all on!"
"I'm a gentleman and I try to conduct myself in that manner."

—Ronnie Garvin

"I'm simply the greatest wrestler in the world."

—Jimmy Garvin

The two Garvin brothers have always been an interesting twosome. In a way, their lives parallel the TV show *The Odd Couple*. One brother, Jimmy, is unruly and messy. The other, Ronnie, is straight as an arrow and clean. The two brothers grew up in Montreal, Canada. Originally there were three Garvin brothers.

Terry and Ronnie were managed by Jimmy, who was just a teenager back then. After a while, the brothers each went their own separate ways. Terry retired, and Jimmy and Ronnie went on to fame and fortune.

Jimmy and Ronnie rarely spoke to each other for a long time, however. Jim was the archenemy of Wahoo McDaniels, who was Ronnie's best friend, and Ronnie despised Precious, Jimmy's wife, who works as his personal valet.

"Gorgeous" Jimmy Garvin is recognized as one of the most vicious wrestlers on earth. With ZZ Top's "Sharp-Dressed Man" blaring in the background, Jimmy makes his way to the ring, wearing outrageous sequined pants, with his long flowing hair tended to by Precious. She also sprays perfume around the ring—sometimes right into the eyes of an opponent!

Although Jimmy *only* weighs 225 pounds, he makes up for it with his meanness and treachery. A blatant rule-breaker, he rarely fights a clean fight. Even more cowardly, he regularly uses Precious to distract the opponents during a match.

On the other hand, Ronnie Garvin is the exact opposite. Always a fan favorite, he uses massive strength to defeat his opponents, who are often the more repulsive types.

Through a mutual agreement, they steer clear of each other. Jimmy has said of Ronnie's friendship, "It's not my fault that my brother chose to associate himself with a worthless piece of trash." And Ronnie said of Jimmy, "I care about my brother, but Precious has no values at all." Hmmm.

Although Ronnie and Jimmy have never wrestled against each other, they have been known to come to each other's aid. In the summer of 1985, Jimmy was in the middle of a brutal war with Dino Bravo and Gino Brito, Junior. During the match, Ronnie surprisingly came to help out his brother. Another time, Midnight Express really ganged up on Ronnie. When they temporarily blinded Ronnie, and he was helpless to defend himself, Jimmy came to his brother's defense. He taught the Midnight Express that dishonesty is the worst policy!

The Garvin brothers have teamed up to teach the Midnight Express a lesson, one that won't be lost on the rest of the wrestling community.

"The Garvin brothers have reunited, with revenge on our minds," warned Jimmy.

"After all," Ronnie chimed in, "blood is thicker than water."

Although the Garvin brothers could be a devastating tag team, only time will tell if they can set their personal differences aside long enough to become a permanent partnership.

RANDY SAVAGE

"He's going to give The Hulkster some trouble for sure."

—Bruno Sammartino

As it stands today, Randy Savage is the top contender to topple the Hulk's reign. There's a certain thinking in the WWF that he's just the man to do it. What was once described as an impossible task now looks within the grasp of Savage. "Hogan-ha,ha,haaaa!!!" is exactly the way Randy looks at this challenge.

Randy Savage was born Randy Poffo. He's the son of former wrestler Angelo Poffo and the older brother of Lanny Poffo, the poet laureate of the WWF.

Before getting his start in wrestling, Savage played professional baseball. He was pretty good. He once led the Florida State League in home runs and RBIs, but he gave it all up to pursue wrestling. He once said that wrestling fits his personality. "In baseball, if you have a bad day, you can't take your frustrations out on anybody. In wrestling, you can beat somebody up."

Beating up people is something Savage does very well. His name alone implies his wrestling style. Although he ranks right there at the top of the most-hated wrestlers list, Randy gets cheers and standing ovations wherever he goes. He has skill, personality, charisma, and perhaps most importantly, *Elizabeth*.

Elizabeth is one of the most gorgeous women ever to go into the ring. Besides being his manager and valet, Elizabeth is also his wife. As nice as this sounds, it does have its negative side effects. With Elizabeth being so beautiful, she often mesmerizes the audience with her great looks. And unfortunately, Savage is the jealous type.

There are many stories about how fans have been so taken with Elizabeth that they have presented her with flowers. The next thing they know, Randy has come tearing out of the ring and is mashing the flowers into their terrified faces.

In fact, Elizabeth is quite a controversial figure in the world of wrestling. The fan magazines are full of letters about her. Some fans say she is a distraction to Randy; she's holding him back. Others say she's in it for her own ego. But most true wrestling fans know that she's a very smart lady. If anyone can get Savage a shot at the Hulk—it's Elizabeth. Stay tuned, fans.

RICKY "THE DRAGON" STEAMBOAT

"A man's got to do what a man's got to do."
—Ricky Steamboat

Not long ago, one of the top wrestling magazines conducted a poll. They asked wrestlers who they most feared in the ring. The usual gang of brutes, bad guys, and cheapshot artists were on the list. But one name was a big surprise—Ricky "The Dragon" Steamboat. What's a nice guy like Ricky doing on a list like that?

The answer is simple. Rick Steamboat's incredible wrestling skills; combined with his extensive training in the martial arts; combined with his intense concentration and inner strength add up to a pretty awesome foe. Steamboat doesn't need cheap tricks. He can do it on pure ability.

Rick was born on February 28, 1953. Wrestling came naturally to him. His father and his brother were both wrestlers. When he got serious about wrestling, he trained with Vern Gagne at his famous school in Minnesota.

Rick made his wrestling debut in 1967—and he was an immediate hit. He won the Rookie of the Year Award. This was before he adopted his martial arts style of wrestling.

Some people say that Rick's style isn't really wrestling at all— that it's closer to judo with a little karate and kick boxing thrown in. But Rick is a true wrestler, and he doesn't use his martial arts advantage unfairly. "The philosophy of karate is a defensive one," he says. "Your opponent must strike first."

Rick is very serious about the philosophical and spiritual side of the Oriental martial arts. He says it isn't enough to train physically. He must be trained mentally and spiritually as well. So he has studied Oriental philosophy and searched for enlightenment. He put it this way: "My Eastern philosophies and training in the martial disciplines have taken the driving wheel while I wait for the earth to turn."

Whether it is because of his philosophy or his ring success, Rick is a happy man. He spends his time with his wife, Bonnie, surfing and driving around near the beach in his Corvette. He only has one sore spot—Randy Savage!

The feud with Savage has been hot for a long time—and it shows no signs of cooling down. These guys hate each other. Their bouts are so intense, the fans pack the halls whenever they meet. But Steamboat has said they don't need the crowds to get "up" for their bouts. They would do it out of anger alone.

You want to see the Dragon breathe fire? Just mention Savage. Then you'd better run!

KAMALA

"The people do not understand the greatness of this man, the powers that he possesses. But once they do, once they see that Kamala the Headhunter is the greatest fighter in the world, they will appreciate him for what he is."

—The Wizard

Drums beat, and the weird, haunting sound of jungle music fills the air. A gigantic hulk of a man struts out to the ring dressed in ceremonial African robes and wearing a hideous mask. He is surrounded by other men, including someone who looks like a masked animal trainer, and a fierce-looking Oriental warrior.

Hey! It's none other than Kamala, the Ugandan Giant! You immediately have to feel sorry for whoever has to fight Kamala, one of the most uncontrollable wrestlers on the planet. But that's what they're paid to do, so you can't feel too sorry!

In Kamala's African country of Uganda, there is an old saying—*"Ninusa mbaya. Hutaki mkula."* Translated from the native Swahili language, that means, "I smell bad. Don't eat me." That very well may save you from being eaten, but it sure won't save you from the savagery of Kamala! Kamala has only one goal in his life—to take the WWF Championship belt away from Hulk Hogan. There are critics who say Kamala will never achieve his goal, because he doesn't know how to wrestle, and although he's more vicious than Hogan, Hulk will always be able to handle him. According to these critics, all Kamala knows how to do is attack and crush people. But they don't say that to his face!

How big is Kamala? He weighs more than 450 pounds, and stands at a staggering six feet eight inches. Having him land on top of you after one of his famous leaps from the top rope would be a lot like having a safe fall on you.

Kamala's career didn't come into its own until the day King "The Wizard" Curtis Laukea became Kamala's manager. King Curtis had always felt it was his personal destiny to see Hulk Hogan fall. According to Curtis, his feelings date back to the day he scaled a mountaintop in the Middle East and encountered the spirit of the Grand Wizard, one of the all-time great wrestling managers. On that mountaintop, the spirit of the Grand Wizard told King Curtis to slay Hulk Hogan. Wait! His story gets weirder.

Well, one thing led to another, and before you knew it, the Grand Wizard's spirit was living inside of King Curtis's body. (And they say wrestling doesn't affect you mentally!)

Although Kamala had won his matches with great regularity under King Curtis, that wasn't enough for the reborn Wizard. Curtis taught Kamala how to crush his enemies by jumping off the top rope.

The end result was that Kamala indeed became a headhunter.

In fact, the beatings became so severe that some wrestlers refused to get into the same ring with him!

In December of 1986, Kamala finally got his big chance—a matchup against Hulk Hogan himself. Not surprisingly, the match didn't start in the ring, but in the dressing room before the official fight was supposed to begin. By the time the fight made it down to the ring, it was an all-out war zone. Although many observers say Kamala won the match, it ended in a disqualification, so the Hulkster retained his championship belt.

The Wizard eventually sold Kamala's contract to Mr. Fuji, but Kamala's number one goal remains dethroning the Hulk. That's bad news for the rest of the pro-wrestling world. They have to deal with Kamala's wrath until he wins that heavyweight belt.

G.L.O.W.

"G.L.O.W.? You want to know what I think of G.L.O.W.? Well, I think it stinks! It's not real wrestling at all. It's completely phony and show biz. You want to know if I watch? You'd better believe it! Every chance I get!"

—anonymous wrestling fan

"The girls look terrific. Who cares if they can wrestle or not?"

—another anonymous wrestling fan

Women's wrestling has always been an important part of the sport. Some of the most unforgettable moments in the history of pro wrestling have involved women. For instance, in 1984, when Wendi Richter defeated The Fabulous Moolah on a match televised live on the cable network MTV, it drew one of the biggest audiences in wrestling history.

Although that match didn't revitalize women's wrestling the way some observers thought it would, it did lead to the formation of a new wrestling federation—G.L.O.W. (Gorgeous Ladies of Wrestling). Many wrestling writers and fans dismiss G.L.O.W. as mere entertainment, because the televised matches feature too much fluff. The wrestlers are featured in comedy skits, a rock video featuring the Gorgeous Ladies often runs during introductions of the matches, and a lot of show-biz gimmicks are used during the matches. Absolutely none of the Gorgeous Ladies are just wrestlers. They each play a character. And sometimes, it appears as if the wrestling matches are supposed to be comedy bits in between the comedy bits they already have. Many wrestling fans are turned off by stupid antics, which are too much like the Saturday morning wrestling cartoon, *Hulk Hogan's Rock "n" Wrestling*.

However, a lot of other wrestling fans, like me, enjoy G.L.O.W. Their wrestlers are not as muscle-bound as men wrestlers, so they're able to exhibit more agility. Some of the G.L.O.W. women are excellent gymnasts, and can jump off the ropes or deliver a flying dropkick *better* than a male wrestler.

Sure, it's enjoyable to watch a 500-pound giant jump off the top rope. But a female wrestler like Hollywood, or her tag team partner Vine, can jump twice as far as Kamala, or even the Hulk! And anyone who says that women aren't as tough as men should watch Hollywood and Vine go at it. Those two street kids, who grew up in the worst slums of Los Angeles, know a lot more about delivering punishment than most men do. They've had to be tougher than men to survive. Whatever they lack in ring strategy is made up for by their manager, Aunt Kitty, who's been around the mats long enough to impart plenty of dirty tricks.

Tina and Ashley, the Beverly Hills Girls, are the opposite of Hollywood and Vine. In fact, they're archenemies. Tina and Ashley are into high fashion and wear expensive jewelry and chic clothes into the ring. These two are becoming the darlings of the G.L.O.W. scene. They appeared on the cover of *Beverly Hills* magazine and act as the Ann Landers and Dear Abby of the wrestling world. They give out advice between matches in their "Asking Ashley" and "Advice from Tina Ferrari" segments.

California Doll is also featured in a talk segment, but it sure isn't anything like an advice column. Her "happy face" trademark sort of sums up her personality—pleasant but your basic airhead. However, real wrestling fans figure she isn't as dumb as she looks. It takes more than a pretty face to stand up to the bouts she's been in. Her wrestling ability is definitely no problem. Sometimes her nice-girl personality gets her into trouble with the bad-girl wrestlers, because they are able to take advantage of her trusting nature and trick her. But her athletic ability and her ring instincts make her one of the toughest women wrestlers around.

Just as Andre the Giant is one of pro wrestling's biggest gate attractions, G.L.O.W. has its share of female hulks. Mount Fuji and Matilda the Hun are two of the biggest women you'll ever see. Like Andre, their size presents an impossible situation for other wrestlers. Matilda and Fuji are virtually unbeatable. Either female giant can beat two normal-size opponents at the same time. In one battle royal, eventually won by Mount Fuji, it took *five* women to get Matilda out of the ring!

The only similarity between the two women is their size, however. Where Mount Fuji loves children, and often visits shopping malls to sign autographs for kids, Matilda is an evil, witchy character, whose hobby seems to be making other people's lives miserable. That's what makes matchups involving Mount Fuji and Matilda the Hun so remarkable—it's truly a matchup between good and evil.

There are many other exciting Gorgeous Ladies in the G.L.O.W. federation, so you should see for yourself whether you like it or not. G.L.O.W. isn't for everyone, but there's a sizable audience out there for top-quality women's wrestling.

MISTY BLUE

"The workingman's ethic is lacking in a lot of today's wrestlers. They all want to be like Richter and Hogan. Glamour and glitter first. They don't understand that fame can't precede hard work. You must expect to break a nail or two to reap any kind of reward."

—Misty Blue

There's a woman in female wrestling who has made it in a very big way. She can drop-kick a wrestler out of the ring a couple of rows back with the best of the men. She is Misty Blue.

Don't let her beauty and feminine charm fool you—Misty adds an all-new definition to the term *femme fatale*. "Deadly" and "cunning" are just two of the nice things her opponents have to say about her.

"I'm the undisputed World Champ," she loudly boasts. Misty Blue is set to knock the world of women's wrestling right on its ear—literally.

"I got involved with wrestling because I love the sport," she says. "I got tired of seeing old, fat, and ugly women dominate it. I want to put ladies back into ladies' wrestling."

Misty's not the kind of person who's afraid of breaking a nail in the ring. She's not in it for money. She's in it for pride.

Misty has said of it, "It's pride in appearance. Pride in performance."

If there's one person whom she owes a great deal of her success to, it's the legendary Killer Kowalski. "I owe all of my success to the master. He allowed me to realize my potential." Fortunately for her, the Killer hasn't passed on his beauty advice to her as well.

Misty's main goal is now, as she put it, "to run the water buffaloes out of professional wrestling."

That's bad news for all those water buffaloes out there. You know who they are—the overmuscled and overweight wrestlers. She has the talent to reshape women's wrestling.

Currently, Misty is the U.S. Women's Champion, as well as the IWF Titleholder. Surprisingly enough, the IWF title was not an earned title, but rather, it was given to Misty for being the finest champion ever.

Despite her small size, she's one mean cookie. Always cunning, she knows what she's doing in the ring. It's almost as if she knows exactly what her opponent is going to do. Killer Kowalski, her mentor, feels this way about her: "She may have my nose, but Misty's awfully smart. She's some tough lady!"

Of course, you always get those hotheads, those starchy, uptight guys who believe women shouldn't be in the wrestling business at all, because wrestling isn't ladylike. But Misty's on a one-woman mission to make sure that women's wrestling is treated with the same respect as men's wrestling. She's got our vote on that one!

DICK MURDOCH

"I'm going after Rhodes every chance I get. I'm going to make his life miserable. Nobody turns their back on Dick Murdoch."

—Dick Murdoch

Dick Murdoch is known as a ruthless anti-American. He is a traitor, if ever there was one, and he's proud of it!

Murdoch wasn't always this way, though. He was once a good American in every sense of the word. He attended West Texas State University, along with fellow wrestler Dusty Rhodes, where they'd go out and party together, and double-date. Unfortunately, he doesn't hang out with his old pal Dusty anymore. Nowadays, his best buddy is Ivan Koloff, a Russian committed to the utter destruction of the American way of life. Why this sudden change on Murdoch's part? Dick put it this way, "There's

nothing about Dusty Rhodes I like. I don't like his ugly face."
Hey, so long as it isn't personal, right?

Dick Murdoch has shocked old friends like Dusty Rhodes by hanging around with people who claim to be against the red, white, and blue! However, some observers feel that Murdoch isn't really siding with our enemies. They think he's just using our country's enemies in a personal vendetta against Dusty Rhodes. The reasons? Obviously, they say, Dick is mad at Dusty for winning the NWA championship three times, while Murdoch has never even won once.

The central figures in this so-called jealousy scandal are Nikita and Ivan Koloff. Ivan Koloff was a Russian defector who came to our shores in the hopes of freedom, democracy, and good hamburgers—things you don't ordinarily get in the Soviet Union. Ivan became a bitter bad guy. But his nephew, Nikita, went straight and teamed up with Dusty Rhodes. So Ivan teamed up with Kremlin Hatchetman Vladimir Petrov and swore to get Rhodes. It made perfect sense that Murdoch would join them.

He has already attacked Dusty Rhodes both in and out of the ring. "I'm going to make his life miserable," exclaimed the six-foot-four, 267-pound Murdoch.

In a way, you can't blame Dick Murdoch. He's been a very important part of many successful tag teams in the past. Along with Rhodes, he's been a big part of wrestling. But time is passing both him and Dusty Rhodes by. In fact, it's a sad commentary on American athletes that both Rhodes and Murdoch, once considered the cream of the tag-team crop, have both resorted to hiring foreign tag-team partners!

Just think about it. Imagine a world in the future, when American athletes have fallen prey to laziness, and no longer train hard, and eat wholesome food, and lift weights. Then we'd have to import all of our pro wrestlers from foreign countries! And there would be no room anymore for homegrown and American-bred wrestlers.

But hey, let's not get carried away. We believe Murdoch is still an American champ underneath. As he puts it: "I can understand holding your hand out in friendship to a foreigner. That's the true American way. We Texas boys are noted for our hospitality."

KEN PATERA

"No one showed me or helped me. I did it all on my own."

—Ken Patera

Ken Patera is one of the most dangerous men in pro wrestling today. If you don't believe me, just ask some of the wrestlers he's put in the hospital!

Ken's most famous move is "The Swinging Neckbreaker." Make that his most *infamous* move. To make sure he wipes out his opponents, he often continues to apply it, even after his opponent surrenders the match.

Believe it or not, Ken Patera has not always resorted to tactics like this to win a match. He once was a good guy. He even attended ultraconservative Brigham Young University. They don't even believe in drinking coffee there! From there, Ken went on to the 1972 Olympic Games in Munich. Not only did he win the

Bronze Medal in weightlifting, but he still holds all of the American records for Olympic weightlifting as well.

After the Olympics, Ken Patera took up professional wrestling, after rejecting offers to play professional football. He was known as the strongest man in sports, and his image was as clean as a whistle.

After being denied chance after chance to fight for championship titles, however, he gave up his good-guy image altogether. He dyed his hair to give himself a new look and started acting downright rude to opponents. Some say he was talked into playing dirty by Captain Lou Albano, before the Captain cleaned up his act. That's when Ken turned to his "Swinging Neckbreaker" more often, too. Ken explained it this way: "Because of my aggressiveness, I do what I feel I have to do in the ring."

Although he is still the strongest man in wrestling, and one of the scariest, Ken trains every day. He realizes that to be the best, he has to stay in shape.

Ken dominates in the ring, as he proved when he was tag-team partner with Big John Studd years ago. Patera more than stood up to comparisons with "wrestling's other giant." But when you ask him why he's in the sport, his star loses some luster. Because, he says, he's only in it for the money. "The money is lucrative," he explains. "I make about a hundred thousand dollars a year." Big bucks. Really. Think about it. Do you know how many sodas you can buy with $100,000? Staggering!

What's the big secret behind his "Swinging Neckbreaker"? Is it a case of superhuman power, dirty tricks, or old-fashioned trickery? According to Ken, "it's nothing more than a full nelson, with my awesome strength behind it."

Fortunately for the rest of the world, he keeps it in the ring!

KING KONG BUNDY

"I'm the biggest event in sports history."
—King Kong Bundy

King Kong Bundy is one of the strangest-looking men in the history of wrestling.

Although certain wrestlers are scared stiff to go into the same ring with him, they all agree that at least it's better than meeting him in a dark alley.

Bundy was born in Atlantic City, N.J., in 1957. He played football and wrestled in college. He once said that college wrestling did not lead him to get involved in professional wrestling, "because the two just don't mix. Amateur wrestling is for wimps."

Bundy weighs an unbelievable 430 pounds. His best maneuver is the big splash. That's where he lands on his opponent and turns him into a pancake. Bundy is not a very quick wrestler. In fact, he has all the agility of a lamppost. But at any given moment he has the power to flatten an opponent.

Not exactly the most cordial of men, after college Bundy became a bouncer in an Atlantic City bar. A bouncer is a person who throws people out of a bar when they become too rowdy. Unfortunately, Bundy became a little too involved in his work. He started to throw everybody out! That's where he got the nickname "King Kong."

Bundy went from one bouncer job to the next and eventually threw Gary Hart, a wrestling manager, out of one of the bars. Hart was so impressed by the way he was flung into the street that he offered Bundy a wrestling contract.

The rest is history.

Bundy admits he's overweight, and he's proud of it. "I'm really a super heavyweight. Face the facts here. Just how many wrestlers out there can match me weight-wise?" he boasts.

King Kong currently can be found in the WWF. He recently gained the fans' wrath by jumping on Hulk Hogan and "squishing" him.

That's Bundy for you. A master of overstatement in every sense of the word.

DANNY DAVIS

"Is referee Danny Davis a superhero? Is he a friend of
the CIA? Does Vince McMahon owe him money? If the
answers are no to all these questions, why has this
man not been suspended? Each week he violates the
basic premise of officiating—that of not being biased
toward one participant."
                              —fan letter from early 1987, before
                                         Danny Davis's suspension

In the entire history of professional wrestling, there has been no
greater villain than Danny Davis. Sure, there have beeen evil
wrestlers before, who break the rules and enjoy inflicting pain
on other human beings. But the sense of fair play in the sport,
represented by the referee, was always there. That is, until
Danny Davis came along.

You see, Danny Davis was a referee for a long time. But he was constantly involved in strange matches. It always appeared that, when Danny Davis was the referee for a match, the wrong team won. He'd be busy in a corner of a ring during a match and turn his back when certain wrestlers completed a legal pin. Then, when the wrestlers he liked would get their opponent on the ground for a second, he'd give a quick three count, and Danny Davis would decide the match.

It happened more than once. Some of the wrestlers who were victimized by Davis's funny business were the British Bulldogs and the Killer Bees. In the case of the Bulldogs, on at least one occasion, they were robbed of the Tag Team Championship by Danny Davis's sloppy refereeing! While Jim Neidhart of the Hart Foundation was being pinned by Danny Boy of the Bulldogs, Davis made sure he didn't see any of it happening. But as soon as the Hart Foundation got the upper hand, Davis made the three count.

It came as no surprise to followers of the World Wrestling Foundation when Danny Davis was suspended for his actions. President Jack Tunney certainly had enough proof that Danny Davis was an unfair referee. To those wrestling fans who really know their stuff, it wasn't all that shocking that Danny Davis became a wrestler soon afterward. And it sure wasn't a coincidence that Jimmy Hart, the manager who had benefitted the most from Danny Davis's terrible refereeing decisions, became his manager.

So now, there's a situation in wrestling where a rule-breaking referee is allowed to wrestle professionally. Davis was suspended as a referee, but not as a wrestler! Due to the peculiarities of the World Wrestling Federation, an arrangement like that could be made. It's legal but a lot of fans are steamed about it! And so are a lot of wrestlers!

As of this writing, Davis hasn't performed well at all as a wrestler. In fact, opponents, most of whom have felt like they were robbed at least once in their careers by a referee, only attack Davis more fiercely because of his former job. Davis seems to expect his tie with manager Jimmy Hart to protect him from the brutality of the reality of ring justice! The plain fact is that Danny Davis is as bad a wrestler as he was a referee, and that he's finally getting what's coming to him.

It's a form of justice to see Danny Davis take a beating match after match, and the fans love it! After all, it does prove that there is some integrity left in pro wrestling, and that the true villains in the sport get their just desserts in the end, after all!

SERGEANT SLAUGHTER

"I walk into the ring, and people shake my hand.
They used to spit on me."

———Sergeant Slaughter

In the crazy world of wrestling, we're used to seeing guys go
from being bad guys to good guys or good guys to bad guys
pretty fast. But the change-around that Sergeant Slaughter made
was so fast that even wrestling experts still can't quite believe it.
The Sarge used to be one of the most-hated wrestlers in the
sport. His famous "Cobra Clutch" was feared by all the good guy

wrestlers. Then one night, faster than you could say "God Bless America," the Sarge jumped to the top of the good guy list.

It all happened in Allentown, Pennsylvania. The way Slaughter tells it, he was there taping some TV bouts. The Iron Sheik was in the bout before his. But when it was time for Slaughter's bout, the Sheik wouldn't leave the ring. He stayed there chanting pro-Iran statements and putting down America. Now Sergeant Slaughter was a bad guy, but he was also a marine—and somehow that night, seeing the Sheik shouting that anti-American garbage got to him. The next thing he knew he was in the ring, wrestling and beating the Iron Sheik. "The fans were chanting U–S–A– the whole time," Sergeant Slaughter remembers. From that moment on, Sergeant Slaughter became the beloved symbol of patriotism that he is today. Just like that.

Of course some cynics will tell you that it seems mighty convenient that Slaughter and the Sheik just happened to be right there together at just that moment—and that is a little surprising that the wrestling promoters just happened to have the Marine Corps hymn all cued up and ready to go—but that's show biz.

Whatever the real story, Sergeant Slaughter is much happier in his new role—and much more successful. He's been made a member of the G. I. Joe Team. A special Slaughter action figure is now part of this popular toy line.

Sergeant Slaughter has also appeared in TV commercials, and he was one of the spokespeople who helped raise money for the renovation of the Statue of Liberty. "There's only one lady in my life and her name is Liberty," he said.

In the meantime, Sergeant Slaughter has also found time to wrestle some of the toughest and meanest wrestlers in the sport. Some of his best (or do we mean worst?) bouts have been against Kamala, Nikita Koloff, and Boris Zuckoff.

When he wrestles, he hands out American flags and plays the role of the defender of liberty. At home, though, the Sarge says he's a pretty laid-back, regular guy. He plays golf. He likes to have barbecues with his family.

Hey, it's the American way!

WRESTLING TRIVIA QUIZ

TRUE OR FALSE

1. The sport of wrestling is over 5,000 years old.

2. Kamala, the Ugandan Headhunter, once ate a live chicken on the television show *TNT (Tuesday Night Titans)*.

3. Andre the Giant once defeated Gorilla Monsoon in a boxing match.

THE CHAMPIONS

4. The only masked Heavyweight World Champion in the history of the International Wrestling Association was:
    A) The Masked Marvel
    B) Mil Mascaras
    C) The Masked Meanie
    D) The Iron Mask

5. Superstar Billy Graham once held the World Wrestling Federation Championship. In what city did he beat Bruno Sammartino to win that title?
A) New York
B) Boston
C) Baltimore
D) Philadephia

6. On which date did Wrestlemania I take place?
A) March 31, 1985
B) April 7, 1985
C) March 31, 1986
D) April 7, 1986

7. Of the following professional football players, which were NOT participants of the Wrestlemania II Twenty-man Battle Royale?
A) Dick Butkus
B) Bill Fralic
C) Russ Francis
D) Ernie Holmes
E) Ed "Too Tall" Jones
F) Harvey Martin
G) William "Refrigerator" Perry

8. Who is the only man to successfully pin Andre the Giant?

9. Who was the only wrestler managed by Bruno Sammartino?
A) Andre the Giant
B) Larry Zybysco
C) Antonio Inoki
D) Nick Bockwinkle

10. Match the wrestler with his nickname:

1. Superstar	A. Koloff
2. Birdman	B. Brutus Beefcake
3. The Living Legend	C. Ricky Steamboat
4. The Barber	D. Randy Savage
5. Macho Man	E. Jimmy Snuka
6. Mr. Wonderful	F. Greg Valentine
7. The Snake	G. Paul Orndorff
8. Superfly	H. George Steele
9. The American Dream	I. Bruno Sammartino
10. Russian Bear	J. Jake Roberts
11. The Dragon	K. Billy Graham
12. The Hammer	L. Koko Beware
13. The Animal	M. Dusty Rhodes
14. The King	N. Harley Race

11. Name the wrestler who was fat, wore a ski mask, smoked a big cigar, and was one of the most hated men in wrestling.

Answers: 1) True **2)** True **3)** True **4)** Mil
Mascaras **5)** C (at the Civic Center) **6)** A
7) A&E **8)** Hulk Hogan **9)** B
10) 1–K 2–L 3–I 4–B 5–D 6–G 7–J
8–E 9–M 10–A 11–C 12–F 13–H 14–N
11) The Destroyer

Scoring: Give yourself 10 points for every question you got
right. Then consult the scoring box below.

If you scored 50 or below, you'd better hit the books—this
one.

If you scored between 60 and 150, you are definitely a wrestling fan with a lot of potential.

If you scored between 150 and 200, you're a real champ—
but something tells us you may be watching too much
wrestling. Better break out the homework every once in a
while!

GLOSSARY OF WRESTLING TERMS

1. National Organizations
• The National Wrestling Alliance (NWA)

The NWA is the oldest established wrestling federation. Its roots go back to 1904, when a group of promoters recognized Frank Gotch as the official world champion. Then, in 1948, five of the major wrestling promoters in the country met to officially form the NWA. NWA matches are seen nationally on WTBS, the Atlantic cable superstation.

• The American Wrestling Association (AWA)

In 1957, when a controversy over a title bout regarding the world champion couldn't be resolved, a group of promoters formed the AWA. Although many attempts have been made over the years to reunite the NWA and the AWA, they do just fine as rivals, similar to the way the National and American Leagues exist in baseball. The AWA features a syndicated wrestling program, "Pro Wrestling USA," seen on many different channels across the country.

• The World Wrestling Federation (WWF)

When another controversy over a title match erupted in 1963, a group of East Coast promoters split from the NWA to form the World Wide Wrestling Federation, now famous as the WWF. Since then the WWF has established itself as the most powerful wrestling federation. WWF matches are seen on the USA cable network, and on many local TV stations. The WWF offers the widest variety of programs, including "TNT," a wrestling variety show, and Hulk Hogan's *"Rock'n'Wrestling,"* a cartoon show.

• World Class Wrestling

On February 20, 1986, yet another federation split from the NWA. This time a group of promoters objected to some NWA rules.

2. Titles, Belts, and Championships

Each national organization has its own world heavyweight champion and a pair of tag-team champs. In addition, the organizations award other belts, such as the WWF's Intercontinental Champion.

There are also many other regional wrestling organizations all over the country, and the world. Some of the more famous regional titles are the Mid-South, Mid-Atlantic, Florida, Southern, and Texas. The oldest regional belt is awarded by Vermont. Its line of champions goes all the way back to 1860!

3. Wrestling Moves

Listed below are some of the most common or spectacular wrestling moves, as well as some other terms used in wrestling.

BATTLE ROYAL: A bout where six to twenty-four wrestlers all grapple in the ring, trying to toss one another over the top rope of the ring, until only one wrestler or tag team is left.

BODYSLAM: Usually applied by lifting an opponent as high into the air as possible, a bodyslam is delivered by throwing your opponent's body flat onto the floor.

COBRA CLUTCH: Sergeant Slaughter originated this hold. It is a variation on the sleeperhold, which dates back to Strangler Lewis's stranglehold. Like the Camel Clutch, used by The Iron Sheik, the wrestler applies the Cobra Clutch to an opponent's head, causing him to pass out.

CORNERMAN: A manager, trainer, or tag-team partner who stands in the corner for encouragement, advice, or other help.

DISQUALIFICATION: A rules infraction that is serious enough to end a match. The disqualified wrestler loses the match, but in most matches, he keeps any belt that was risked in the match.

DRAW: A match that ends without a winner. If the time limit ends before a match ends in a pin or a submission, it's a draw.

DROP-KICK: A term used originally in football, college wrestlers brought the drop-kick into pro wrestling in the late 1920s. It's executed by jumping high in the air and then planting both feet into your opponent.

PIN: When one wrestler holds an opponent's shoulders to the ring canvas for the referee's count to three.

THE FLYING BODYPRESS: The most popular finishing maneuver in wrestling today. The wrestler climbs on the ropes, often the top rope, gains his balance, and leaps off onto his opponent.

SUBMISSION: A fall that happens when one wrestler forces another to surrender to a painful hold he can't escape from.

LEGLOCK: A leglock is applied with the legs to an opponent's legs, resulting in pain and loss of circulation.

PILE-DRIVER: The most dangerous wrestling maneuver. A wrestler traps an opponent's head between his legs, lifts him in the air, then drives his foe headfirst onto the floor.

SQUARED CIRCLE: A slang term for a boxing or wrestling ring.

SUPLEX: A move, often executed with the feet, delivered to the chest, and designed to knock the wind out of an opponent.

TURNBUCKLE: The part of the ring where the ropes are attached to the corner ring posts. The turnbuckles are filled with foam rubber padding to keep wrestlers from getting hurt, and to feed George "The Animal" Steele.